How To Make Cash Fast

Fun and Legal Ways to Earn More Money In a Weekend

Judy Helm Wright & Megan Herring

© 2013 by Judy H. Wright, Family Educator and Author in
Residence at Artichoke Press, LLC
2400 West Central
Missoula, MT 59801
ISBN-13: 9781491250211
ISBN-10: 1491250216

Web site: www.ArtichokePress.com
Parenting Blog: www.AskAuntieArtichoke.com
Abundance Blog: www.WelcomeAbundance.com

For additional parenting, wellness, life-story writing, end-of-life
books and programs please see our website or contact us
directly.

ARTICHOKE PRESS, LLC

DEDICATION

Dedicated to all the entrepreneurial spirits who know how to assume personal responsibility for their lives. They not only think outside the box, they build a better box.

There's a Harvard University study that says 85% of the reasons for successful accomplishments are because of a can-do attitude and consistent small action steps.

Only 15% are because of technical expertise.

If you want to make extra money or become rich, you can. Just do it! We are pulling for you.

Forward

Yikes! The rent is due and the car just broke down. You are just about making it, but you need more income and less outgo. You have already donated plasma and sold your computer on Craigslist, so what do you do?

There are really only two options:

1. Spend less

2. Earn more

Giving up McDonalds will help you save long term, but if you need instant money to pay bills, you need instant solutions. There is a ceiling on how much you can save by cutting down, but the sky is the limit on how much more you can earn.

In the global economy right now, times are tough. It is hard to find a job or career that will provide for needs as well as a few wants.

Do not feel that you are unsuccessful or lack motivation because you can't find the perfect job or business. It is easy to get discouraged and down when finances are tight.

One solution is to "create a job(s)." Most of us need multiple streams of income.

It is important to decide what you really want and what you will be willing to sacrifice to reach that goal. Almost all extra jobs require a commitment of time, energy and consistent action.

"True unhappiness is giving up what you really want for what you want right now."

Seed Money To A Secure Future

Some of the ideas included in this little book require some "seed" or starting money. You can get that by spending less and finding ways to be more frugal. If you have a specific goal for the money you are saving, you are more likely to do so.

If you save money by not eating fast food for a month, earmark the savings for a weed edger to start doing yard work, which you can use to make more money when you need it. Next you could use the money you make from landscaping on summer evenings to buy a lawn mower so you can get more jobs.

$200 More in a Weekend

You want something that can bring in at least $200, not another job. There are so many ways to create and earn that doable amount that you will find yourself thinking of how to leverage the margins and expand your reach.

Why $200? The difference between most people who declare bankruptcy and those who are able to make it through a rough financial time is only an extra $200 a month.

If you get behind $200 in January, the next month you are twice as behind, plus now you have interest added on. It just keeps spiraling downward.

Ideas, Opportunities, Options

According to Ramit Sethi of "I Will Teach You To Be Rich," **the #1 barrier to people earning more is finding an idea**. Everyone loves the thought of earning $1,000+/month. But when you ask them how they might do it, they suddenly stop, confused about which idea might work—or even guilty that their idea could never be good enough to charge people for.

As we move into a global economy, the label you want to have is "Problem Solver." Figure out a problem that someone has and how you could solve it, and the money will follow, as long as you ask for it. Do not devalue your talents, skills and expertise.

There are hundreds of ways to earn extra cash that are legal, ethical and fun. Thousands of people go outside their comfort zone every week in order to bring more income into their households.

Assume Personal Responsibility

The first steps to financial independence are the most difficult. It takes enormous effort to look inward and recognize that we are responsible for financial choices we have or have not made in the past. Being broke is a choice! So choose to do something about it.

It would be so easy to blame someone else. Maybe your parents or their parents? Or how about the economy and the politicians? They made laws that had an effect on our wealth or lack thereof, didn't they?

We can't change the past, but we certainly do have control over our future and our finances. Make the decision today to choose and then consistently follow a path that will lead you away from lack and debt and toward financial security.

Multiple Streams of Income

One of the best ways to insure a secure future is to have multiple streams of income coming into your home and bank account. If you want to start your own business, you can also benefit from tax advantages and deductions offered to businesspeople. But, you may just want to increase the cash coming in monthly to provide a cushion of security.

The happiest people are those who have options. They know how to develop a plan b, c & d. The following sections are filled with great ideas that you can adapt almost immediately.

Make a decision to take action on just one idea and move forward to that goal. You will be surprised at how many will doors open, mentors appear, and opportunities abound.

What is Your Dream Job?

Figure out what you would love to do and find a way to do it part-time or occasionally. Life is too short to be bored, broke and beaten. You and you alone have the choice to create cash legally, smart and fun. While you are earning more you will also be learning more about your talents, skills and genius.

Table of Contents

- Art Show

- Bucking Bales

- Gleaning From Farms & Orchards

- Paint Street Numbers

- Recycle Scrap Metal

- Bikes and Billboards

- Personal Trainer

3. Making Money Inside

- Rent Out a Room or Garage

- Rent Out Your Couch

- Tell Fortunes or Read Palms at Parties

- Respite for Care Givers

- Clean a House

- Deep Clean a Kitchen

- Organize a Closet

- Party Planner

- Decorate For Holidays

- Brand Ambassador

- Estate Sale Coordinator

- Tee Shirts for a Cause

- Clutter to Cash

- Editing and Proofreading

- Selling Sporting Goods

- Local Sales with Facebook

- Design for Dollars

- Word Press Wealth

- Monitor Websites

- Sell From Your Online Virtual Store

- Freelance Work

- Write an eBook

- Hidden and Unclaimed Money

- Sell Your Time and Voice as a Remote Customer Service

5. Making Money With Arts & Crafts

- Turning Antiques Into Cash

- Hair Halos

- Selling Stock Photos

- Steampunk

- Festive gift baskets

- Knitting and Crocheting

- Paint a Picture

- Teach Origami

- Make Wind Chimes

- Spray Paint Shirts

- Iron On Designs

- Tie-Dye Clothes

- A House for the Birds

6. Making Money With Food & Beverages

- Cater or Waiter

- Discount for Advanced Payment

- Gluten Free Desserts

- Birthday and Wedding Cakes

- Food Truck

- Craving Cookies?

- Mixologist

- Pick Up Groceries

- Teach Cooking Classes

- Roxy Candy Pebbles

- Tea Parties for Toddlers

HOW TO MAKE FAST CASH
FUN AND LEGAL WAYS TO EARN MORE MONEY IN A WEEKEND

HOW TO MAKE FAST CASH
FUN AND LEGAL WAYS TO EARN MORE MONEY IN A WEEKEND

ACKNOWLEDGMENTS

A huge round of applause for the young interns who show up to learn and stay to teach. Kristine Quint is the very able editor, publicist, and assistant who put this little book in your hands.

CHAPTER ONE
TOP THREE WAYS TO EARN $200 THIS WEEKEND

1. Sell "stuff" on Craigslist, eBay, Etsy or your online classified listing

It is amazing what people are looking for and are willing to buy. You bought it once, and so will they. Look around your house and office and spend a few minutes taking a photo and write a compelling review listing all the features, benefits and reasons for selling.

This week, I sold a camera that I hated because I couldn't figure it out, a long dress coat that I had bought at a thrift shop, and a teapot that once belonged to a relative.

Bingo...I made $187.

I am comfortable having people coming to my home, but my friend Tee always has people meet her in the Costco parking lot. We both ask for cash.

2. Sell at craft and art shows

In order to make a profit from a handmade or wholesale product the markup is four times what it cost you to produce. If you buy a bunch of earrings online for $1.00 then you have to sell them for at least $4.00 to cover costs and make a profit.

Many new entrepreneurs forget to figure in their time. If you make jewelry while you are watching a movie, you can figure a lower hourly "wage." If what you are doing is labor and time intensive, you should be figuring a salary to cover your costs.

My friend Kay loves to take photos, and she has them printed on cardstock and sells them as cards, singly or in a package. She buys the envelopes wholesale and can usually sell $300 to $400 worth in a heavily trafficked art show. She also sells them online but figures in the cost of mailing and time to go to post office etc.

It is getting competitive to get into art shows and craft venues, so plan ahead and have your products ready to go.

PS: Stand up and greet every person with a smile. You want them to buy your products as a gift, so give them the gift of being proud of your product.

3. Do services for others

In my blog posts at http://www.WelcomeAbundance.com, I am going to go into greater detail about the many ways you can profit from doing something you like to do that others don't. Most people take it for granted if they are handy, organized, good cooks, know how to clean a house, wash windows, plan a party, clean a garage, detail a car etc.

Trust me, not everyone knows how to do those things, and would be willing pay to have you perform your service for their benefit.

My nephew has a small pickup and advertised *"Have Muscles & Truck-Will Help You Move."* He worked during the week, but could usually pick up a couple of hundred dollars on a Saturday helping people move from one house to another. He even sub-contracted with his girlfriends to help people pack for a fee.

See Solutions Where Others See Problems

What could you and your family do to bring in an additional $200 this weekend? Brainstorm some ideas, set an intention and get to work. We all have choices and those who are happiest in life are those who choose to be pro-active and go after their goals.

CHAPTER TWO
MAKING MONEY OUTSIDE

Whether you're washing windshields, detailing cars, or selling the surplus veggies and greens from your garden at the local market, these ideas will help you get out of your home or office while still being productive.

Mowing for Money

Most owners of small yards pay $25.00 per week to be on a regular lawn maintenance schedule. That includes mowing, edging, and hauling away the clippings. Any other services like weeding, planting, prune trees, or fertilizing could be charged at an hourly rate.

You need a lawn mower that works well, a lightweight edger, strong back, good work ethic, and the ability to knock on doors and find work. Work fast, wear headphones and listen to motivational books, and you will soon run your own landscaping business.

Washing Windows

This is one of the easiest and most appreciated gigs you can do. Make up flyers and paper a neighborhood or take out a small ad in the weekly paper. Give a discount if the homeowner gets three of their neighbors to do their windows on the same day.

Generally, window cleaning costs $3-$7.00 per pane. Our son charges $5.00 a pane so he does not have to go to the house to give an estimate. If you have a 1,300 square foot house with 20 panes, the price would range from $40-$140. This is inside and out.

He says, "I love those 'miracle cloths' for making windows sparkle with nothing but warm water. If the windows are really dirty or greasy, use a bit of Dawn liquid dish detergent and then rinse with the cloth dipped in warm water and dry with the other one. Make sure you get in all the corners."

Use a little hustle, personality, and politeness, and you can easily make an extra $400 in a weekend. Enough to make the rent, a concert or a car payment and still a few bucks left over to make you feel like an independent entrepreneur who is in charge of his or her life.

Windshield Washer

This could not be easier now that "miracle cloths" have
been invented. Use damp one to wash the window and a
dry one to make it shine. Position you and a buddy in a
long line of cars waiting to exit an arena, airport or major
parking lot, and wear tee shirts that say:

"Sparkling Windows--$2.00 Each"

Most people will have you do the front and the back and
offer to hit all of them for $5.00. When they give you the
money, make sure you smile, say thanks, and hand them a
business card for detailing cars at the workplace.

Gold In Them Thar' Hills

Many people who have yard sales or estate sales do not
separate the good jewelry from the cheap, and you can pick
up sterling silver chains, pendants and pins, as well as 18k
gold ones. Take a small magnifying glass and look for
markings on the jewelry. You can sell it by the ounce to
brokers, who then sell it to be melted down for gold and
silver bullion.

Leanne from the Gold & Relics Company, located in
Canada says, "We used to go gold prospecting for extra
cash, now we teach others how to do the same. We use a
metal detector and it is certainly not impossible to go out
for a weekend and earn $200 and maybe a lot more."

Feel free to take a look at her website and to contact
Leanne for further information at www.goldandrelics.com

Walk and Sit the Dog

Folks are busy. Sometimes, they're too busy to even walk
their golden retriever down the street and back.

For $10 bucks a time or even more, you could walk
someone's dog or a few peoples' dogs at one time. It'll add
up. And if you love dogs, why not add watching them
while the owner's are away to the list?

Dog kennels can be scary places, and in most cases dogs
are locked up for hours in a cage. They're also more likely
to get sick in a kennel. Offer to stay at the house with the
dog so the owners can get out of town while you play with
them, scoop poop, feed them, and fill up the water bowl.

Detailing Cars

Get your business cards ready and go into large office
buildings. Set your prices for inside detailing at $35.00 a
car or for four cars from the same office for $100.00. Ask
permission to connect your electric vacuum and the water
hose. You will need a small vacuum with an extension cord
that reaches the cars, and you may want to have them move
the car to a spot close to the front of the building, especially
near a water spigot where you can attach your hose.

Your kit should include "miracle cloths," Armor All, a
small spray bottle of soapy water and one of clean water to
rinse the gummy spots on the doorframes, and some spot

remover. Take out the floor mats and wash them with a stiff brush to get all the debris out of the crevices. If you do a good job on this, you will establish a route and most people will have you detail the interior every month.

Farmer's Market

Grow extra vegetables, fruits, or flowers and share them at the market. One neighbor grew only pumpkins, but she did artwork on them with acrylic paints and sold them like crazy.

Another money stream at farmer's market is to do two venues, and split the profit with the other grower. Or, you can do convenient gleaning and go to someone near the end of the show and offer him or her a price for his or her remaining goods. You then take their goods and go to a busy intersection and sell them. Make sure you have a big sign a block away so they can give you the five dollar bill when you hand them the goods.

Parts are Parts

If you have an old motorcycle or car that is impossible to sell or is no longer functioning, then sell off the pieces of equipment that are still in working order. Take it apart and sell engines on eBay, or even the windshield wipers. People are looking for new parts for their vehicles and you can provide for them, and yourself.

Yard Sale With A Purpose

The most successful yard sale I have ever attended was
near the college, and the girl had posters showing the
textbooks she needed to purchase with their prices. When
she made a sale she made hash marks on the poster. Of
course most of us told her to keep the change, or made an
extra contribution. Being smart should be rewarded!

Art Show

Be a "Vendor Relief Person." Go early, introduce yourself
to all the vendors, and set up a schedule of when you can
give them a lunch or bathroom break. They are usually
willing to pay someone to help set up & take down their
booths, too. Charge $12-15 an hour and make sure they
know you know enough about their product to double that
amount in sales while they are gone. After they get to know

and love you, many will accept your invitation to man the booth alone if they have other commitments.

Bucking Bales

Look in the paper under farm and ranch equipment and make friends with the sales people. They will give you tremendous leads of farmers who need immediate help. This is back breaking, but muscle building work. Most farmers pay by the hour but offer room & board during haying season. If you are a smart cookie, you negotiate a piece price. You will work harder and the farmer will be impressed and give you a great recommendation to his cohorts down at the local coffee shop.

Gleaning From Farms & Orchards

Many orchards will allow you to glean what is left on the trees and vines after the machinery or pickers are through. You can take the produce to the Food Pantry and feel good about yourself, or you can take the produce to a place where you can sell it and feel good about paying the electric bill.

Paint Street Numbers

It just takes paint, stencils and a willingness to walk neighborhoods to earn $10 to $40 per curb painted. http://www.HowToAdvice.com can help you start your own curb-painting business. Our grandson did this as his Eagle Scout project and he turned out to be a great young man, so it must be a good idea.

Recycle Scrap Metal

Some salvage yards and recycling centers pay for scrap metal and they pay good prices. You'll need a truck to lug the metal around. **http://www.RecycleInMe.com** lists scrap-metal buyers and the latest prices.

My friend Henry, who has his own carpet cleaning business, has a scrapping and recycling gig. He checks Craigslist list daily for free computers, televisions, and electronics, the older the better. He takes them apart for the copper, gold, silver, and aluminum bits and pieces. With a pair of needle nose pliers he pulls out the gold plated pins, cast iron parts, and copper wire. Even old television and computer cords have a copper middle, just strip off the rubber on the outside.

He separates the metal into piles and takes them to the refiner to have the gold melted down or to the recycling center to sell the rest. While most of the kids his age are off drinking beer or listening to heavy metal rock bands, he is investing in precious metals.

Bikes and Billboards

People are always looking for ways to advertise their business and with an increasingly warming planet; they are especially looking for greener alternatives.

That's where Richard Palowski stepped in and came up with Bike Billboards. He and his wife created billboards that attach to bikes. Not only does it catch eyes, but it's also a green alternative and a great way to get some exercise.

The business has grown and today www.bikebillboards.com sells Richard's design to people looking to get ahead in the market place. You are obviously one of those people, so you can either use his design for your own purposes or you can do advertise for other businesses. You could charge up to $100 for the advertising space and all you'd have to do is ride the bike around and make some money. Even better, hire someone to ride the bike for you while you collect and split the profit.

If the bike doesn't seem like a good fit, start your own way of selling advertisements. Create an advertising car complete with funky signs, or just offer your services to stand outside of businesses with colorful signs. There are always creative ways to tackle a new business angle.

Personal Trainer

Got killer abs and an addiction to exercising? Pay for your gym membership by becoming a personal trainer from home. People are trying to get fit and lose weight, especially after holidays, so take it upon yourself to be their guide and very loud encourager.

For around $70 an hour you can make up to $210 for a weekend. Think of all the endorphins. All you have to do is market your business, do some research on fitness, and go for it. Don't be reactive to life, but be proactive about your future. Make a decision to control your own destiny.

Kenny Pena of Evolve Fitness needed some extra cash after Hurricane Sandy destroyed his car in the fall of 2012. "On the weekend I do small group training out of my backyard," he explains. "I make $70 an hour and do two to three hours straight early in the morning. I start at eight A.M. and I'm done by eleven with $210 in my pocket. It's now starting to grow into a Saturday and Sunday thing, so some weekends

CHAPTER THREE
MAKING MONEY INSIDE

You don't have to push a lawn mower to make money. Instead of veg'ing out in front of the television or staying up all night playing video games, how about making some money while you relax?

Rent Out a Room or Garage

I have a couple of friends who rent out a room in their basement to traveling nurses or truck drivers. These are single people who have been screened and vetted before renting. The nurses work three or four days a week and then go back home, so they just need a quiet place to sleep. The truck driver is in town about one weekend a month and he not only rents the room, but half of their garage to store his car. That is some sweet money for sharing a fridge and garage with someone occasionally.

Rent Out Your Couch

The couch is no longer a place for angry spouses to spend the night; it's a cash making heaven! There are plenty of people who may need to crash for the night or a few days and would be more than happy to take up residence on a couch.

Mike Fingado, General Manager at Tred.com, started his own company by, among other things, renting out his couch on Airbnb. "Eventually," he says, "all my work paid off into a full time job."

Renting out the couch for $75 a night might seem a little crazy, but think about it. At a hotel, customers usually don't have a hospitable host or even breakfast, and it's usually twice as much to stay in good areas in a big city. Personally, I'd rather crash on the floor than stay in a two star motel where bed bugs might bite up my legs. Think of all the crazy stories you'll hear from the people prancing through your door, too.

Respite For Care Givers

With more and more Baby Boomers comes the typical "sandwich generation." Many inter-generational families need a break from trying to sandwich a life in between caring for kids and elderly parents or a housebound family member. And frankly, the patient could use someone new to listen to his stories, laugh at his jokes, and enjoy his presence.

You can register with an agency or you can place an ad in a senior center. Most senior companions make an average of $15 an hour. Be very honest, caring, and provide references.

Clean a House

We all want a clean and organized house, but we don't want to clean and organize it! Hellllllllo. Opportunity is knocking. Put your ad under 'resumes" on Craigslist. Make up a flyer and post it at beauty shops and gyms. Take someone with you the first time to be safe and just split the money.

People actually pay more if you can "Green Clean" with all natural products. The going rate is $20.00 an hour per person with a three-hour minimum.

Deep Clean a Kitchen

This is worth $150-$200 and includes cupboards, drawers, and appliances. Inside and out. Top to bottom. Client supplies drawer liners, storage containers etc. Or, you can have a brochure of cleaning products you have available. You buy wholesale and sell to your client for retail.

Organize a Closet

Once again, everyone thinks they will do it eventually, but probably not. The going rate is $20.00 an hour, with a three-hour minimum. It helps if you have an eye for color and style and can be kind, but firm with the hostess.

Make three piles: Consignment, Donation and 'What in the world was I thinking when I bought that?' The rest can go back in the closet in an orderly and organized way. If the hostess has not worn it in a year, out it goes.

One organizer I know will deliver the donations to the battered women's shelter as part of her price. She then mails back the tax-deductible receipt to the hostess.

Party Planner

Did you know that people pay for this? Yeah, and a lot. Your fee can be inclusive (includes all games, prizes, food etc.) or just for certain parts of the party. Our friends with one child were tickled to pay someone $200 to act as hostess and head honcho for a sixth birthday party.

Laura Yamin is a Media Strategy Consultant who has a side hustle as an event planner when she wants more cash. "I have learned to position myself as the go-to-the-day-of-the-event assistant. I work with the organizer as their right hand girl who can manage the crisis without breaking a sweat. I typically earn a couple hundred of dollars for a day of work."

Leave flyers and business cards at day care centers, beauty shops and gyms.

Decorate For Holidays

Big bucks here if you get clientele lined up before the holidays. The Jones's tree has to be the best and brightest in the neighborhood. Once again, make sure you are charging enough to make a profit. You are not a non-profit organization.

Make your brochure by going to http://www.fiver.com to have a graphic designer put it together, or make one yourself. You want something that will be dynamite and show your decorating skills. Then plaster the office buildings with it. Many businesses want someone to do the decorating and no one on in the reduced staff want to volunteer for the duty.

Brand Ambassador

All products have to get into the public somehow, and they aren't going to magically sell themselves to consumers. It's the job of a brand ambassador to promote products to people either door to door, on the street, or in private consultations. Usually, you'd slam the door in a sellers face, but these people can actually make some money and it is a great way to supplement an income.

"Anyone that is punctual, can smile, and has a generally good attitude (or can fake it) can be a brand ambassador and make $200 in a weekend," says Gordon Vaughan of Mogul Solutions. "I worked with many teachers that do this work in the summers for supplemental income, loads of students, and young professionals that needed to supplement their first job."

Check out websites and Google "merchandiser" and see who is hiring in your area. Once you become a merchandiser or brand ambassador for one company, they will recommend you to other companies. Many merchandisers work for numerous companies and get wages and per diem expenses from all of them.

It's a great way to earn some money on the weekends instead of wishing you had more and sitting there pondering what's to be done on Monday.

Estate Sale Coordinator

This gig is often associated with Assisted Living Centers or realtors. Who is downsizing, moving into assisted living or to live with a relative? It's a lot of work, so be sure you get at least 25% of the proceeds. Family might fight over grandma's gravy ladle, so be prepared to do some peace negotiations along with having a donation pile, yard sale pile, and then estate sale offering.

Tee Shirts for a Cause

You are smart enough to think ahead.
www.Vistaprints.com will do tee shirts for as little as $6.00
each. If you want inspiration about making a business out
of this, go to the library and check out *Life is Good: Simple
Words from Jake and Rocket* by Bert Jacobs. For five years,
Bert and John Jacobs traveled the East coast, selling their
tee shirts in the streets and in college dorms.

They lived on peanut butter & jelly, slept in their van, and
showered when they could. By August of 1994, with a
combined sum of $78 in the bank, the brothers considered
giving up the ultimate road trip. Then they created the
cartoon character Jake, and he showed them the way.

Today, the Life is Good brand is dedicated to spreading the
power of optimism and helping kids in need through its
community of optimists. For more information, visit
http://www.lifeisgood.com.

Clean Out Files and Shred Old Papers

We have stuff in our files that we have not looked at in
twenty years. If we look we have to make a judgment and
either pitch it, or put it somewhere else. So, we don't look.
It is worth $50 to $100 to have an unbiased person bring
out the paper file and force me to make the decision to toss,
re-file, scan, or shred.

One word of caution: do not let the paper come into my
hands. Once I have physically touched it again, it becomes

more valuable somehow and I want to save it, study it, or tell you the back-story. Be merciless.

Label and Photo Scribe Photos

Charge $20 an hour to go through boxes and dressers and put labels on the backs of pictures, or a flat fee of $250.00. Encourage clients to have the photos in piles according to "Themes" such as ancestors, family trips, school photos, etc. Many baby boomers are more comfortable with a project fee rather than a by hour cost.

 It should take you about six hours to scan and caption the photos and give the family a DVD that can be duplicated. You can charge for adding music to the disk or any other services you might do.

Most families don't have a clue who is in the picture, or the back-story of the event pictured. There is an old African saying that "Every time an elder dies without sharing the story, it is as if the library has burned down." If you need help or assistance, please go to http://www.MontanaStoryKeepers.com.

Trade For Tutoring

Not all income needs to come in the form of cash. Decide what you want and why you want it, and then start trading. Tutoring is a perfect example of using talents you already have to teach someone something they would like to learn.

Or, you can charge for cash. Priya Mohan, a Marketing Analyst at TeliApp Corporation, says that depending on the expertise of the tutor, you could easily earn $200 or more in a weekend. "Tutors who teach college and high school level courses earn from about $25 to $75 on average!"

Scrap Out Computers & Electronics

Computers and electronics are full of valuable metals. For example tower cases are usually made of steel and/or aluminum. The CPUs, RAM, motherboards, and PCI' all contain gold.

You can offer to take outdated computers off the hands of a building or school doing upgrades. A friend consistently finds junked computers in the free ads.

If you can repair and update them, do that and make more money that way. But if they are not worth updating and you can't sell the components on Craigslist, then scrap the parts and pieces and you will have some extra cash in your pocket.

Housesitting

Leaving the house unattended always comes with a certain amount of risk. Will the flowers die? Who will make sure the cat is fed? What if we leave milk in the fridge? All those questions won't even need to be asked if there is a person, such as you, willing to house sit.

Get paid $10 an hour cleaning up the yard, watering plants, and doing basic chores everyday while the owners are away. It'll pay off and it's fun to explore the ways in which people live.

Daycare Professional

The people who work with the very young and the very old are the angels in the world. These people have to have a calling or they are better off selling shoes at Wal-Mart and so are their clients. If you have the patience, loving heart and ability to make a difference in the life of a vulnerable person, then perhaps this is the perfect part time profession for you.

Please do not consider calling these highly trained professionals "babysitters." As a parent educator, I know and respect those who do this important work.

Carpet Cleaning

This is from my young friend Henry who took a bad situation and really made it turn out excellent. He was working for a company who didn't keep their promises to customers or employees. He realized that he could do it better, faster and more honestly. Went to a bank and family with a business plan, bought equipment and worked 7 days a week to pay off the loans.

He does an outstanding job and I am happy to recommend him to other landlords. You will find his website at http://www.MissoulaCarpetCleaningKings.com. He and his wife have multiple streams of income and they are the kind of people you want to help succeed.

Improve On What's Already Good

"Ever since the success of Jibbitz I've looked at things with an eye towards improving on something that's already good," says Kally O'Mally. "My idea was washable chair covers for the most commonly found steel case chair that we have at the hospital. I made and sold about fifteen of them, for $25 to $30 for the set."

Take a leaf out of Kally's book and improve on what is already good. If you know a good car detailer but you also know how you could do it better, why wait? Fill the niche that's needed.

CHAPTER FOUR
MAKING MONEY ONLINE

Already working a couple full time jobs, or just want to be able to kick back in the shade on your porch when you've got some spare time? Why not make money while you do it? These ideas will get you earning money online faster than a Google search.

Answer emails

The Internet provides so many moneymaking opportunities, but not all of them are legitimate. Reading emails from the comfort of your own home is one way of doing it right, plus you can get the money instantly, which is also great.

Conduct a Google search for "Paid emails" then select the service that interests you most.

In most cases, you will be required to sign up and be a member. But do not pay to work. The sign up process is usually free of charge and there are others that offer bonuses just for signing up.

Cash from Craigslist

In addition to selling extra junk (I mean treasures), Craigslist is a wonderful way to find work. Be sure to check all of the different categories, because often the poster will not know how to word the ad so that it reaches the correct prospects. You also need to post your talents under "Resumes" so that people like me can find immediate help.

Do you know what sells better than anything else on Craigslist? Furniture, appliances and electronics. So if you are looking for some fast cash, check out the free stuff advertised in the paper or put on the curb as college terms end and sell it. Pure profit.

Write articles, blog posts, reviews

If you are a competent writer and can work up an article or blog post in less than an hour, then this is the gig for you. Karen Cordaway, for example, is a freelance writer who regularly contributes to a popular website and has her own blog, and this is how she earn her living.

Check out http://www.iwriter.com or http://www.elance.com. Plan on not having your name on the product and that it will go through copyscape. This is usually a good gig if there is one particular niche you can write about again and again because if you are fast, accurate and a good writer, clients will ask for you.

Fiverr

Fiver is a place for people to share things they are willing to do for $5.00. You will find funny, bizarre as well as excellent candidates to do social marketing, graphics etc.

Deanna Balestra is a realtor who needed a few extra bucks when things started to slow in the market. She always had a passion for writing and storytelling, but she never followed up on the idea before because of competitive jobs that had little pay. Dabbling in graphic design as well she figured she might as well try and make some sort of money with her talents as a writer and designer.

Using fiverr.com (http://fiverr.com/deannabalestra), Deanna began to write blogs for people, short stories, and design websites. After seeing the positive feedback, she started her own website where she offers stories and articles to the public (http://www.deannabalestra.com/). Soon she plans to write some fun ghost stories and even some full-length novels.

If you have a talent for the written word, get out there and sell your work. Don't be afraid to take up a keyboard and start stroking away (as in typing not petting your computer). The money will follow.

Use Your Voice

If you have one of those great radio voices you can make some serious cash. Many companies hire "voice over artists" to narrate a video or commercial. Check out www.goodvoices.com

Search Engines for Jobs

www.Indeed.com is a great site for finding quick gigs. Another one that was recommended by friends is www.cooljobs.com Never forget, Google is your best friend. Be very proactive in Googling ideas and then networking with other entrepreneurs. Most people are willing to mentor as long as you ask a few questions politely and send them a thank you note.

Tech Savvy Graphic Design

Websites are hard work, and it's even harder when you have no clue what you are doing. Luckily there are people who have the ability to work with new computer technology and have extremely artistic ideas.

Take Jessica Greenwalt for example. In high school, she helped design websites and worked on graphic design projects for a number of people in her area. Once she began to attend California Polytechnic State University, she realized that she needed to make some more cash and now that she was in college, it was time to step up her game.

Looking up adds for graphic designers in the school newspaper and keeping an eye on school bulletin boards, Jessica began to build up a portfolio and impressive resume. Soon, she was able to pick and choose her clients as she worked in a freelance capacity using Photoshop, Illustrator, and InDesign.

If you know how to use the software and have a knack for design, stop screwing around with old photos and apply for some graphic design jobs. Just remember to start small and slowly build up not only a clientele, but an impressive portfolio as well.

Earn on eBay

The first thing you need to remember is that you are there to SELL, not BUY (unless it is a really, really good deal and you can resell it at a profit). Get registered on eBay and establish a payment system like PayPal. When you set up a virtual store as a buyer, make sure you follow every one of the policies and rules.

You can sell your own stuff, stuff from clients (usual commission is 40%), or you can buy things online that are close to selling out and then list them on eBay while you are waiting to get them.

Valuable Virtual Assistant

Most solo-entrepreneurs are overwhelmed with all the tasks they face in a day. If you are good at organizing, scheduling, research, and anticipating what the boss needs, then you can work from anywhere in the world as an administrative assistant. Try to find one niche to specialize in and you will get more clients and referrals. If you are good and can provide references, you can charge $20-$40 an hour. Some prefer to charge by project, rather than hourly.

Our realtor has a VA who does social media, designs ads, schedules open houses, arranges publicity, and writes a blog post under his name every week. She lives 500 miles away and he has never met her face-to-face, but he pays $300 a month to make sure everyone online knows, loves and trusts him. She has six clients and averages about ten hours a month, spread out in little bits and pieces on each client. She got her training from http://www.virtualassistant.com. Another site to check out is http://www.ivaa.com. This is the International virtual Assistant Association and they offer a certificate program and other helpful information so you can succeed.

Barter for Business

I know another woman who barters her haircuts for social media postings and an occasional blog post. Win-Win. Think hard, what can you do easily that is hard for someone else?

The www.Goodbuygirls.com started their business and remodeled their store by bartering, trading and exchanging with others who were starting out. They could do graphics and websites and they needed plumbing and painting.

Affiliate Marketing

As an affiliate, you simply refer people to other sites and earn a commission every time a sale is made. It can be as easy as including a link in your emails or as complicated as a big affiliate launch. Affiliate marketing is the basis for MLMs or referral marketing, so it is governed by some pretty strict rules to keep the scammers out of the field. Play by the rules and make residual passive income.

You can become an affiliate for major stores like Target, Wal-Mart, or Amazon, as well as very specific niche sites. For instance, http://www.ArtichokePress.com has an affiliate program, so if you bought this eBook through the recommendation of a friend, they will get a commission. If you do a lot of Internet marketing, you will want to check out http://www.commissionjunction.com and http://www.jvzoo.comand http://www.clickbank.com.

Clutter to Cash

Jamie Novak, author of "Stop Throwing Money Away," has a great suggestion. "Whenever you sell anything online, you are required to create a username for the website. I start my name with the letter A or the number 1 and tailor it to the items being sold. For example, if I'm selling a bundle of classic books, I'll create a username like 'ABookworm." Starting the username this way guarantees that your listing comes up first when potential buyers search for your products.

Jamie uses http://www.Etsy.com to sell her unused craft supplies as well as her art products. We have found that we can shop on Etsy.com but hit the button for local artists and then connect personally and save shipping costs. Good to keep the cash in the community. Other online options are http://www.Artfire.com, http://www.Zazzle.com, http://www.Threadless.com, and www.cafepress.com.

Editing & Proofreading

As authors, we can either pay an intellectual editor to proof read and make red marks, or we can submit our work to http://www.Elance.com or http://www.Fiver.com and find a person who will do it fast, accurate, and cheap. Long gone are the days when major publishers had editing teams.

Now, most books are self-published by independent small presses (Hurrah for http://www.ArtichokePress.com) and have to keep the prices low, because the margins are thinner.

Selling Sporting Goods

When the kids outgrow the soccer shoes and the baseball mitt is gathering dust in the closet, log on to http://www.PlayItAgainSports.com and make some fast cash. I have found that I make more there than selling it on Craigslist.

Local Sales With Facebook

One of the major drawbacks to selling goods online is the trouble of shipping and handling. Many people are not sure how to take the money and it is easier to either let it sit in the garage or donate it to charity. However, one of my daughters started a Facebook page and invited 25 local friends to join her. They then invited their friends and people could upload a photo of an item, asking price and other details. It felt safer and once again the cash circulated in the community.

Design For Dollars

If you are good with graphics or just have Photoshop, you may want to consider advertising your design business. Here is a sketchy ethical deal that while I don't approve, did happen. An intern took a design job of a new logo for $2000 from a business his dad worked with and then submitted the idea to 6 fiver gigs. He then offered the client the top three designs and they chose the one they liked best and happily paid him the full amount.

Word Press Wealth

Working with Word Press has made blogging so easy. They offer templates and you could easily do it yourself, but most people do not want to. In order to create websites, you need some basic HTML and the ability to see how the big picture is linking behind the scenes. It is absolutely imperative that your business has a web presence. Most people are not tech savvy and just want someone else to do applications for them. Judy's husband's plea at tax time is to just have http://www.Artichoke Press.com earn as much as we pay the web designer.

Monitor Websites

This gig is actually a great little moneymaker for a friend of ours who was downsized and needs to bring in extra cash every month. He charges a flat fee of $50.00 per month to monitor and maintain all websites he has built in the past. Customers are grateful to have someone familiar with the system and are confident with his ability. It takes him about 20 minutes to monitor each one on a bi-weekly basis and he has over 100 customers. You do the math!

Download free monitoring software at http://www.internetuptimemonitor.com and then start contacting businesses that need or have websites.

Sell From Your Online Virtual Store

Dropship products you buy from wholesaler. Essentially you are doing what every other retail shop does—Buy wholesale and sell at a profit.

If you can find a wholesaler who will sell to you and you can retail the product, you keep the difference. You don't want to be stuck with a lot of inventory, so ask if the wholesaler will dropship for you.

You can Google wholesalers or ask people at art shows where they get their products. If you have a friend going overseas, have them pick up some products and then you sell them in your community.

The usual markup is 4 times the cost of the goods. That gives you some leeway if you have some damage, to pay overhead and duh! Make a profit.

Freelance Work

Many easy-money stories will suggest putting your creative skills to work by freelance writing, doing design work, etc. I don't recommend this as a feasible way to make quick cash as it takes time to build up a clientele, even if you're well connected. Freelance work often pays pathetically little until you're well established and collecting paychecks can require the muscles and intimidation skills of a "Guido."

For some reason, people don't place as high a value on creative skills and many have no qualms about asking you to work for free. That said, freelance work could be an excellent way to maintain your skills while developing a network for a real job. http://www.FreelanceJobs.org has an extensive list of freelance opportunities in many different areas.

Write an eBook

Colin Grussing is a self-identified "serial entrepreneur" in New Orleans. He suggests writing an eBook to earn some extra cash, particularly a subject in high demand but with little information. He suggests how to do a yard sale. "How to yard sale gets 1,000,000 searches per month and has zero ads. Make the book a bargain, and aspiring yard salers will snap it up faster than a Beatles 45."

Hidden and Unclaimed Money

If you are like most people you probably have money that you don't even remember that you have. Before you donate clothes to Goodwill, go through the pockets. Lots of hidden bills are left there.

Many older people have memories or have heard stories of banks failing and so do not trust that they can get their money when they need it. When cleaning out for an estate sale, a friend said she found hundred dollar bills in books and in the sides of cereal boxes. Her mom was Japanese and had gone hungry during a war.

Our daughter Debra financed her vacation this year by researching "lost or unclaimed money" online for her state.

Much to her surprise, she got a check for $700 from a forgotten savings account and a tax refund.

Sell Your Time and Voice as a Remote Customer Service

If you are organized, have a good voice and friendly disposition you can move a quiet place in your home into a job. Call centers cater to businesses that don't have someone to answer their phones 24 hours a day. The calls come into an 800 number but then are routed to individuals who work from their homes.

You will need computer skills and software in order to do this effectively. Most companies are legitimate and offer an hourly wage or per call premium. Some, however, are not honest and want you to invest in their equipment and training before going to work for them. If this is something you think you would like, check out http://www.callcentercareers.com for more information.

CHAPTER FIVE
MAKING MONEY WITH ARTS AND CRAFTS

If you normally like to spend your free time doing arts and crafts, whether painting or making gift baskets, capitalize on your creative time by making some money while you're at it.

Turning Antiques into Cash

The amount of old worthless items sold out of peoples' garages every year is just mind-boggling. They do say one person's trash is another's treasure, but sometimes items don't fall into that category. At least in this circumstance the old idiom rings true.

There are certain items or antiques that are prized by collectors. Unfortunately, a lot of people don't consider their old belongings to be antique worthy and so they just throw them out or sell them for a dollar at a yard sale. This is where you come in and capitalize on their mistake.

Cody DeLong and his wife would go to antique and estate sales and sell their products on Etsy. They would sell four to five items per week, but always have more they needed to sell, until their friend gave them the idea to take their products to a flea market. "We took advantage of it and sold out of almost everything we had laying around that first weekend and just continued to go to estates sales on Friday and Saturday, and then flip on Sunday at the flea market. We easily turned $200 into $400 to $600 each weekend."

You can go to a yard sale spend $50 on old merchandise and then turn around and sell the same goods for up $200 or $400 at antique shows. Just do some research, know what you're looking for, and don't be shy to sell your own junk.

Hair Halos

Girls always want ornaments of some sort in their hair; it also helps to have some thick full locks. If you got the creative bug then set it free by making hair halos. These fun accessories are made from hair extensions and creating a band that can easily be put onto a lucky girl's head. Bands can be decorated either by a strand of braided hair, roses, shiny plastic diamonds, or just a piece of ribbon. Depending on the quality of the hair extensions your using you can sell these easy crafts for up to $3 or $4.

Of course, if hair extensions seem a little too hard to handle then you can still make fun hair accessories by decorating some cool headbands and selling them for $10 each. A thin band of leather or ribbon elaborately decorated could help to bring in some extra dough while you have some crafty fun.

Selling Stock Photos

People take millions of photos everyday. With hundreds of editing apps and advanced cameras on cell phones (as well as the regular camera that everyone seems to forget nowadays), many images are just too good to be true. That's where some cash can be made.

Even if you have never picked up a camera before, it's not very challenging to learn the process of editing breathtaking photos. You can sell these photos on the Internet or print out for a friend as stock photos. Consumers with empty picture frames are looking for that new stylish photo that pops, so why can't you provide it for them? A number of websites sell stock photos where buyers can choose and download a photo.

Grazina Snipas launched a website called Pico Images where people can sell photos they take every day for cash. "We know most people have smartphones with cameras and a lot of people are actually pretty great at taking photos," she said, "so we thought it could be a nice revenue stream for non-professional photographers."

A few cents or dollars for a photo may seem like small change, but in reality this adds up quite quickly when billions of Internet users are involved.

Steampunk

A new subculture has emerged, and it is booming. Here's the rundown: heavily influenced by literature and engineering genius, Steampunk is becoming the new hot thing. Set in the midst of the industrial revolution during the Victorian Era, steampunk focuses on innovation and rebellion. Movies, books, and comics have already hit shelves and the genre is only growing.

So how can you get involved? There is a huge market for steampunk crafts that represent creative technology with a Victorian sheen, such as mechanical birds or dragons. You can either create your own piece from scratch or you can take some modern technology such as an old phone or boxy mp3 player and just add some metallic paint or more scuffs.

These little crafty works of art can rake in some cash from small amounts of $5 to, depending on the project, even larger amounts. All sorts of steampunk materials can be created from costumes to jewelry to novels. Do some research, and become a part of the movement whilst making some cash.

My friend Linda who owns http://www.thesteampunklady.com didn't find her niche in life till she was 60 and her grandchild remarked about how she could use up some of the stuff in the garage. Bingo! Big money.

Festive Gift Baskets

Mother's Day, Christmas, Birthdays, Easter, there is always a holiday somewhere around the corner that requires a gift. Chocolates, teddy bears, fruits, perfumes, cologne, or basically any other item can be easily added to a colorful basket purchased at the nearby thrift store.

Gift baskets can sell anywhere form $15 to $100 depending on the goodies within and how much you're willing to work on your presentation.

Jodi Bigby sold gift baskets as a side gig in college. "I would get baskets from craft shops and thrift stores, spray paint them silver or gold, filled them with all sorts of stuff; cologne and perfume, chocolates, coffee, teddy bears, fruit, etc. They sold for $15 all the way up to $100. I even created and printed a catalog and set up in the main student center on the days when vendors would come in to sell at the university."

Sell these bad boys through the newspaper or stand outside stores or airports, just go for it. I myself made $1,000 in one day selling raffle tickets for 3 gift baskets at $1 a ticket when raising money for cancer research. Easy gifts for busy people are in hot demand, so provide.

Teach Origami

Paper cranes are so cool. One of my friends made a ton of them out of colorfully patterned paper and gave each of us one. Mine happened to be blue and green with a paisley pattern.

Learning how to do origami is challenging and the art takes a lot of practice. If you have nimble fingers and a creative mind then why not pick up the traditional Japanese art form? Once you learn origami you can either sell your pieces or you can spread the joy of folding around and teach classes.

Step out of your comfort zone and take on some students, you won't regret it and neither will your wallet.

Knitting and Crocheting

Needles are a great tool for a number of projects and aren't just for grandmothers. A number of fun products can be made through knitting and crocheting from little dolls to scarves, hats, socks, and gloves.

Take it from me, I love knitting and in high school I made a number of colorful hats that I sold for $10 each giving me a decent income for the movies or an occasional lunch date with friends. It's simple and a fun activity you can pick up while sitting on the couch watching your favorite TV show.

While transitioning from couch potato to entrepreneur, pick up some needles and start working on creative projects.

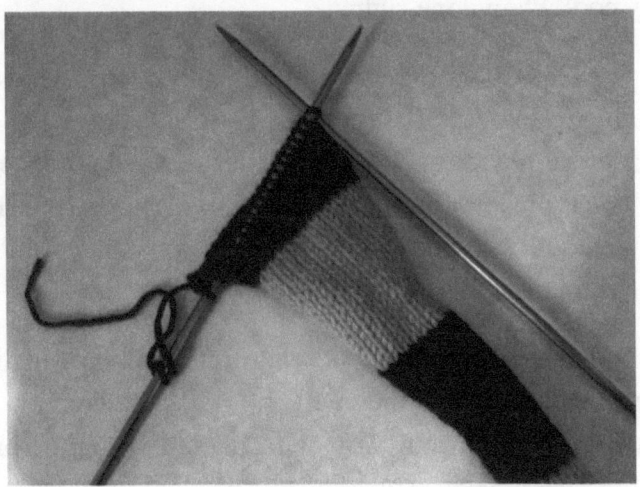

Paint a Picture

Selling art on the street is a great way to make some money and you really don't even need to be an artist to do it. If you have an artistic friend that is willing to split the profit 50-50, become business partners selling the goods.

Gorgeous landscapes to colorful abstracts can all be sold on the street for a good price, and if your friend or yourself has some real talent you could jack the price up to $50 or more. Original artwork can give you a heavy pay off if you do it right.

Make Wind Chimes

A summer breeze just doesn't feel the same without the soft noise of wind chimes (or maybe it's the obnoxious wind chime that ruins the moment). Either way, wind chimes are pretty cool when done right.

What's even better are hand-crafted wind chimes. These could be made out of old recycled bottle caps or even pieces of stained glass. Little treasures that would once be trash could make a fortune for you if used properly. Why not create unique wind chimes that any consumer would love to purchase?

All you have to do is string up your fun ornaments in an intricate pattern where they will collide when the wind starts to howl. You could use bells, medallions, glass balls, anything that makes a sound when smacked together.

If you really want to make some music then collect different sized objects that will give a different tone to your chimes.

Spray Paint Shirts

Spray paint isn't just for sketching out a quick anarchy sign on a wall. It's got a pretty bad reputation, but in truth there is a lot you can do with a can of color. For one, why not create shirts?

I used to do this all the time, and still do. Using cardboard or painters tape I create a fun design on an old shirt, or one that I picked up for cheap. Next, using a fun color or series of them such as lime green and bright pink, I start to spray over top of the design. Let it dry for a few hours outside, take off the tape or cardboard stencil and presto, I have a hand-designed tee with a bit of an edge to it.

This may seem like just a fun little project, but I'm telling you there's some money to be made. Stores are selling pre-spray painted shirts for $30 to $40 dollars each, why not make your own and sell them?

Tell your customers that they're one of a kind and up the price, or sell them at a reduced price and get even more people to buy them. Just remember to wear a mask when creating these masterpieces.

Iron on Designs

There are a number of ways to create a unique and out of this world item of clothing. One of my friends in high school started up a business selling shirts that sported iron on designs or transfers. Being an artist, he drew out his own designs and sold them at the People's Market downtown and to friends. After leaving for college he stopped the business, but he made some good money while it lasted.

You can do this, too. Iron on transfers can be put on shirts, purses, pants, or any other material. These items could be sold for up to $20 depending on the materials being used and the quality of your designs. Sketch something out and see what you can make of it.

Fancy Nail Art

Nails are tricky and doing your own nails is even harder. My mother owns a hair salon and her nail technicians get a ton of customers who really just want to get their nails painted in a fun and interesting way.

If you go onto tumblr.com there is even a whole feed dedicated to fancy nail art from people's favorite TV shows and movies, or just ultra cool looks.

If you're an artist and don't mind working with hands, then start painting some nails. Salons charge anywhere from $30 to $40 for professional nails, why not reduce the price and do them yourself for others while working out of the house? The process is fun and you're getting some money. Instead of watching re-runs get out the nail polish and get to work on someone's nails.

Tie-Dye Clothing

Dude, tie-dye is so chill bro. So many colors on one shirt! I myself have a pair of tie-dyed skinny jeans that I made during a Chemistry class.

The truth is a lot of the time, people actually go out and buys tie-dyed shirts for around $20 or more. But, they could actually save a lot of money if someone would find time to make rad tie-dye merchandise. You could sell those babies quickly down at a market somewhere, or even sell them over the Internet!

A House for the Birds

I love birds, and it's great to give something back to them, like a birdhouse. The problem is many homeowners want a really pretty birdhouse that will look more like a decoration out in the yard as opposed to a home for a nesting wild animal.

By decorating a birdhouse with paints or even building a unique one yourself you could give these homeowners what they desire. Depending on the quality of your work you could sell these little mansions for up to $15 or more.

Birdhouses at the store cost around $15 to $40 so you could even up the price if you have the fan-base to do so. Create a Facebook page, a clever name, and see where you end up.

CHAPTER SIX
MAKING MONEY WITH FOOD AND BEVERAGES

One of the great things about customer service is that you can not only earn money at an hourly or contract rate, but you can also earn tips. It's also a creative way to network, meet new people, and show off culinary skills.

Cater or Waiter

You may be unable to cook, but that doesn't mean that you can't make money through food. Get some friends together and start up a catering service, one cooks the other drops off the food. You can work weddings, office parties, birthdays, or any other special event you can think of.

If you don't want to cater, you can also work as a waiter. Put together an application, go to a few restaurants, and see if they need any new servers. It's that easy. You may make minimum wage, but if you work hard and put on a positive go-get-'em attitude you could make a heap load of tips or get a raise.

Even being a waiter at special events could make you some quick cash for only a few hours of work. Serve guests at fancy weddings or take your servicing power to funerals or birthdays.

Discount For Advanced Payment

Although my friend Jennifer charges her catering clients 50% before the event and the remainder at the event, sometimes she can get them to pay it all upfront. When she gives them a price she will often ask them if they will be willing to pay all before the event for a 20% discount.

Gluten Free Desserts

Everyone is trying to lose weight these days. Pills, surgeries, odd diets, gym memberships, it never seems to end. So, why not take advantage of the craze? Gluten free desserts are both delicious and nutritious—or at least healthier than that funfetti cake.

Invest in your project; buy some gluten free cookbooks from a second hand bookstore, or from Amazon or just Google some recipes online for free.

Next step, start cooking that scrumptious something that you are creating. You can then sell this masterpiece to all those dieting people with a sweet tooth for a dollar each, or more depending on how magical your ingredients are even more. Seriously, gluten free is the new thing; take advantage of the fad and make some extra cash.

Birthday & Wedding Cakes

For those of you who have, up until this point, been too busy watching Food Network and Cake Boss, here's your chance to put all of that "important" research to good use. Decorated cakes are always in demand and it always helps to be able to bake them, as well. Fun letters, edible ornaments, and any other creative feature works well on a hand crafted cake.

If you're really good then make it a full time gig; take some pictures of your work, make a website, create a Facebook page, post flyers, and even enter yourself on Craigslist or the local newspaper. It's all about marketing. Get out the icing and put yourself to work.

Food Truck

Food doesn't have to come from a five star restaurant or from a questionable food chain. Why not take food mobile? On campuses all across the country food trucks can be spotted, selling delicious goodies from crepes to tacos.

If you know how to cook and have the resources to purchase a food truck, go for it. Even with a full time job you can still sell your goods on the weekends or later at night, making the extra bucks you need.

Come up with a menu; create a Facebook page, and start selling your delicious mobile foods at special events or on the street corner.

Craving Cookies?

Bake sales are so scrumptious. Getting homemade cookies and granola bars is one of my favorite treats in the world, and it usually supports a good cause, too. Learn from this fundraising technique, and start up your own home made baking business.

First, come up with some delicious recipes that make your mouth water. Second, figure out a place to create your goodies, whether it be your kitchen or a rented out space. Third, contact anyone that needs to know about your business say food officials or friends who just can't get enough of your sugary perfections. Fourth, sell.

Michael's Story

Like any 15-year-old kid, Michael Adams needed some money. Sure, maybe it wasn't for groceries or gas, but movies and bowling are important in a fifteen-year-old's life.

Unlike any regular fifteen-year-old, though, Michael sought to put his love for cooking and his talents as a to good use.

He started making cookies and energy bars from his home kitchen and sending them off to others to sell at markets. He created business cards and banners to help market his business and took the bake sale to the next level.

His advice: don't plan out an idea and then never act on it. Just do it and see what becomes of it. You can plan every detail until the world ends, but if you don't actually go out and start selling your product it's never going to happen. Find some of your Grandma's old recipes and sell, sell, sell.

Mixologist

Kids, if you're reading this then skip over to the next part, you're too young to be partaking in this venture. But if you're over twenty-one, then feel free to try out this idea.

Mixing drinks can be a very difficult task, but there always needs to be some sort of expert at any large social gathering. If you put in some time researching how to make the perfect cocktail, you could become a mixologist.

Create a signature drink or stick to the old favorites, either way you will be the man or woman of the party. Get fancy, add in some cool bar tricks like spinning bottles or pouring drinks behind your back. This is an excellent way to get some tips and it's a bit more challenging for you.

Pick up the Groceries

I was intrigued a few years ago when my grandma and I were discussing how life has changed so much throughout the years. Back in her time gas was only a dollar a gallon and there were candies that were sold for only a nickel. Not only that, but there were also kids that would take your groceries home for you after you bought them so you wouldn't have to break a sweat. Sometimes all you had to do was give them a list and off they would go buying your goods and you'd just pay them when they got back. Now I'm wondering why not bring that back?

Workers don't want to have to pick up groceries before going home, they want to relax. Why not give them that opportunity? Start picking up groceries for the elderly and working class. Not only is it great for the community, but you can also charge interest to cover gas and to put money in your pocket.

Teach Cooking Classes

I am a terrible cook. Trust me, I burn literally everything I touch. I've been looking for a place to go to learn some cooking techniques so that I may be able to make something other than Top Ramen.

A lot of people are just like me, but if you're lucky enough to have the cooking gene, instead of being jealous I'll give you this idea: teach classes.

Take out some of your greatest recipes and get a group together for a few hours every week, teaching them the fundamentals of good food. Dreadful cooks will be worshiping you after teaching them the wonders of a delicately cooked steak or perfectly diced tomato.

Roxy Candy Pebbles

Roxy Klein has always loved art and of course, who can't resist the allure of delicious candy? At a young age when she was playing with sand art, she thought of candy and how delicious it would be to have candy art.

Through research and hard marketing Roxy was able to take her candy making business to the next level and now sells her product at trade shows.

How can you get involved? Contact Roxy at www.niftycandy.com and start selling some candy art. It's easy, delicious, and pain free. All you have to do is purchase some candy and sell it at special events or to friends and family.

Or you can think of your own type of candy creation. Just be sure to research some ideas and invent a new a tasteful way of making some cash from candy.

Tea Parties for Toddlers

This is a fun way to demonstrate manners and social skills and still have a great play-date. If you have a restaurant that is usually pretty slow in the afternoon, think about setting up classes for manners or tea parties.
Maybe the kids will listen to you about talking with their mouths full.

CHAPTER SEVEN
MAKING MONEY WITH
ENTERTAINMENT

Everyone loves an entertainer. Cash in on your flair for performance!

Play the Piano in Hotels

So you know how to play the piano? You sit at home on the keys enjoying a bit of peace and quite with that monstrous book of charts? Why not trade out your home for a hotel lobby and make some fast cash?

Many a hotel has a piano player quietly playing in the corner and if you're shy no worries, you're just providing background noise that calms and soothes not playing for a massive crowd at Coachella. Just walk into a hotel ask to see the manager or owner and see if they are willing to hire a piano player. You can either see if they will pay you or you can play for free, putting out a hat for some tips.

Either way your making some money and doing the same thing that you would have done if you were hanging out at home.

Background Music

There's a lot to be said about an instrument and some talent. Take my friend, for example. She's been studying violin since she was a little girl, and through high school orchestra met some other kids that were good at playing a tune. They took to hotel lobbies and the like, and were hired by a number of people to play music at different events. She didn't charge much, but it put some cash in her pocket, and she got tips.

Find a place that is hosting an event and ask the coordinator if they would be willing to pay you for your musical expertise. Or market yourself through flyers and Facebook, create a fan base, and start booking some gigs.

Sing at Weddings & Funerals

If you've got some vocal chops, put it to use. Usually, those people are the ones putting on the happiest or unhappiest of events…a wedding or a funeral. You could be paid anywhere from $200 to $300, depending on how long you would be singing, travel arrangements, how good you are, etc.

Turn those pipes into gold, or in this case, green bills. All you have to do is bring some attention to your singing voice, talk to others, and set up some gigs.

Singing Telegrams

Dressing up as an elf, clown, or leprechaun may seem a bit crazy, but with a catchy song you might just make someone's day. Singing telegrams is a great way to earn some money especially during a holiday. You can advertise your little project through flyers, a Facebook page, or just through word of mouth. Friends, family, random people, get out there and spread the love that is dressing up and singing a theme song to that special someone.

Sam's Story

Our 16-year-old grandson sings with a barbershop quartet of middle-aged men. Around the holidays they do singing telegrams and can deliver flowers or gifts along with a melody.

They have even lined up businesses that use their services as a thank you to their clients. About the same price as a bouquet of flowers and much more memorable.

How about you? Do you have a great voice? Think of the possibilities.

Plug In

Playing an instrument takes a lot of talent and ingenuity. If you can get yourself a good reputation and a few great gigs, it's possible to take the hobby to the next level.

Jeremiah David is a musician who plays gigs both with bands in his area and with his own band, Face Yourself. Using an amp and his voice, Jeremiah sings at bars and other venues throughout Seattle. At times he just plugs into random outlets.

If you're able to make some good music, then there are a million ways to make money. Go to venues and sell your music, make money.

Start up a Band

Mike Godoy (vocals), Ian Rico (guitar), Andrew Bushong (bass), and Cedric Anderson (drums) are all members of the growing metal band, Equinoxx (https://www.facebook.com/Equinoxxtheband?fref=ts). They started out playing local gigs and have now moved on to play at the famous Whiskey-A-Go-Go as well as opening for bands such as Dokken and Uli Jon Roth.

Seriously, these guys know what's up. Starting out to make some extra cash and have some fun, they're now recording their first EP entitled "Edge of the World."

Follow their example, if not for making it big, then at least for making money and having fun. Get some friends together and spend your Saturday night on the stage instead of in the crowd.

Strum on the Street

Everyone loves an acoustic guitar, whether it's played in a crowded stadium or on the street. If you know how to play, or you want to learn, then pick up a guitar and get out there.

Leaving your case open you can pick up a few bucks in cash here and there from the friendly pedestrians that pass you by. Start out with a few songs you know well and you may not make much, but after awhile your talent will grow and so will your set list.

You'll get paid more for doing something you enjoy. Find a corner and start strumming.

Be a Mime

Attention all actors! Get out your black and white face paint. Become a mime. Working as a mime is always a fun and entertaining job, not only can you make people laugh and smile with your invisible boxes, you can also earn some money. Either on the street or at a party, mimes are entertaining and it's a great way to get up, get out, and have some fun.

Juggle for Cash

There are many talents that can get a person some cash super fast and in a fun, maybe odd way. Example: if you can juggle. take your circus act to the street corner or to a birthday party and make some money from your talent.

Some parties will pay you up to $10 an hour to keep the little kiddos entertained or you could work for tips on the street. Either way, trade in your odd tricks for cash, take some fun pictures of your act, post them on the internet and see who responds.

Build a Parade Float

Parades are always fun. You may think that they only happen a few times a year, but if you live in the city. college campuses are always having little things going on. Sororities and fraternities make floats for fundraisers, homecoming involves a number of floats, and of course you have all the holidays. So why not make a parade float instead of watching them slide down the street?

Charging by the hour or by how great your end product is, decorating parade floats is a great way to make cash. Business owners don't have time to build a float for their company, but they are looking for someone who does.

Make some time, get out the paint and duct tape, brainstorm, and using a little ingenuity and creativity become the toast of the parade.

Mascot

You've got spirit, yes you do, now let your personality shine through a costume and be a mascot. If you're outgoing you could be the crowd pleaser, dressing up as a company or sports team's mascot. Meet children, sign autographs, and take pictures.

Street Performer

If you walk down Hollywood Blvd. in LA, you'll see a number of people dressed up as Spiderman, crumping, drumming on garbage cans, basically entertaining the masses that walk by to check out the Chinese Theatre. Not only are they having a good time, they have found the time to head out, figure out an act, and make some money.

You can do the same thing. Performing on the street can be a great way to make a few extra bucks. Do some internet research to figure out an act, or think of something completely new and exciting. Bottom line: get up, act out, and perform.

Body Part Model

Usually, modeling is associated with the full package; a nice shapely body with a good face that the camera loves.

But, if you have a part of your body that you think is camera ready why not become a body part model?

There is always a need for hands that can model watches, feet that show off high heels, lips that shine with gloss, or even eyes that pop.

Getting involved isn't that hard. Find a professional photographer to take pictures of your beautiful body part, make a portfolio and then attend open casting calls or send your photos into a company. There's no telling how much you could get paid or how far you could go.

Party D.J.

Are you the person who always groans at party tracks with terrible taste? Then make your own mixes and get paid for them. Take your iPod or mp3make some cool tracks and then start working parties. You may not get paid much, but you can listen to your own music. If you're really cool, you could even download some software that allows you to edit songs or create a mash-up. So many possibilities…

Balloon Man

I love balloons and as a young child, animal balloons were my favorite, especially the puppy ones. Parents love to see a smile on their child's face and balloon animals, or balloons in general, are a great way to make that happen.

If you know how to make balloon masterpieces (and aren't afraid of loud noises), then maybe selling these is the way to go. Giving out balloons for a buck or two will make a child's day while working the job.

Perform Magic

The unexplainable has always fascinated people. If you've got some tricks up your sleeve, take them to the street and impress some unsuspecting onlookers and put on a magic show.

The latter will involve a great deal of flyers, Facebook use, word of mouth, and serious work. If you don't get the information about your magic show out to people they won't appear out of thin air. Prepare your act and sell it, whether you're on a stage or on the sidewalk.

The Art of Fortune Telling

Palm reading, crystal ball staring, and hand holding methods are great ways to see into a person's future.

The first step is to create your character. Please don't put on a wacky gipsy accent unless you're looking to be a comedic act, just be yourself with a bit more flare. Be dramatic and act out your part, and practice on your friends or family members before taking your show to a fun festival or the street.

You could charge anywhere from $2 to $5 a person depending on how good you are. All you have to do is have some fun and entertain folks. Just don't be cruel and try and predict anyone's death or anything, that's just wrong.

CHAPTER EIGHT
MAKING MONEY WITH TRAVEL AND ADVENTURE

Swimming Instructor

Swimming is a skill that many take for granted. Everyone can swim, but they had to learn sometime.

If you know your way around a pool or if you used to be on the swim team, here's your chance to earn some money. Take your friends' kids or open up to the public and teach them the ways of the water.

Give out some swimming lessons for $10 per hour in the pool or even more, depending on where you're teaching and who shows up.

Outdoor Guide

The great outdoors. It's a place of spectacular beauty where one can be free and answer the call of the wild. Or it's where you end up lost in the middle of the woods unable to read a simple topography map.

For the safest and most panic free situations it is best if one is able to hire a well-trained guide, in most cases a local.

That's where you come in. As the person who lives in your area, you know the best spots, and it's no fun keeping those sacred places to yourself when you can show them off.

Start up a guide service. Market yourself to out-of-staters and show them a good time for a little mullah. They're willing to pay if you're able to commit some time.

City Guide

Why not show off your city? Those annoying tourists who can be such a treat to watch may be where your next paycheck comes from if you become a city guide.

Like outdoor guides, you're a local who knows the best places to get a slice of pizza or see a show. Tourists are begging to have someone show them the way in a city where street names and the city culture is foreign. Help them out and get some money for doing so.

Charges for city tours can go up to $100 a person if you're out for a while and do a good job. Put on some walking or driving shoes and show off your city.

Haunted Cemetery Guide

Everyone is looking for a spooky adventure now and again. Cemeteries provide an easy way to give out a few screams and, if you know some history, a bit of an education as well. You could start up a business by guiding people through them. All that is needed is a bit of showy star power and research into who is buried at the cemetery and why they are there. Backstories are always fun to hear and if you get it right, people will come time and time again.

These tours could even become a more somber affair during the day when people are looking for more information about the place instead of a heap of ghost stories. Beware, this requires a good deal of research, but the internet is here to help. Use Ancestry.com or look up old local obituaries. With the right marketing effort you could charge up to $20 or so for a good tour.

Be a Driver

I always see people posting on Facebook that they need a ride somewhere. Sometimes there's not a shuttle service, or in other cases a carless friend just needs to bum a ride home for the weekend. Either or there is money to be had.

On long road trips drivers can usually make quite a bit in gas money, and if you have a car with great MPG, then you're already set up. Or, you can throw your name into the yellow pages or put some adds up so that travelers know that you are able to offer your services as a pleasant and professional driver.

Not only will you make some money from them, but you could also make some tips if you handle bags and gear.

Give Travel Advice

Adventurers are always looking for advice from locals and fellow travelers. Going out and making that information available for a little bit of money is a great way to meet new people as well as fatten your wallet.

If you want to get professional you could even start up a small little travel agency. It doesn't have to be big, it just needs to get the job done. Make some money and if you're enjoying the travel agency, make it into a career.

Take People Rock Climbing

There's a certain fascination that goes along with scaling a large rock wall and a great amount of daring. Lots of people, though, have no idea how climbing works or how to set up gear safely. Take some tourists or adventure seekers out with you the next time you go .

Set up a group on Facebook or create a Twitter account for your business. Bring groups out to the most popular outdoor climbing spots and teach them not only how to set up gear, but how to belay.

Most outdoor adventure experiences cost up to $100 a person and that adds up quickly once a business starts to gain headway. Make some new friends and start bringing people out to the rock wall.

Teach Skiing and Snowboarding

No offense to skiers, but I love snowboarding. Of course it did take me quite a few tries to stop falling on my tailbone every one hundred yards. I needed a good instructor, as does anyone trying to learn a new sport

Taking lessons at a ski hill can be an expensive endeavor, costing almost $50 for a two-hour session at some ski

resorts. Instead of being a mountain bum all day, why not make some cash doing what you love?

Take on a group of new skiers or snowboarders and teach them how to move through powder, or just how to move at all. Don't let the big resorts suck up all the new learners, find a friend's friend that needs a little bit of extra coaching. and bring them out for a day on the slopes.

Teach to Surf

Surfing is a great way to get in touch with the ocean and your paycheck. If you're the type who surfs from dawn to dusk and tracks in more sand than green, maybe it's time to rethink things through. You can still do what you love and make a bit of dough; just turn your passion for surfing into lessons for others.

Surfing lessons on the coast can cost anywhere from $50 to $100 per person. It's crazy how much money can be made. Travelers are intrigued by surf culture and they want to get involved, but they don't even know how to wax a board. Take these people and help them out a bit, what's the harm of having a few more people surfing the waves? Let someone else become a beach bum, you can enjoy your time in the sun and make money too.

Underwater Tours

SCUBA diving is one of my greatest passions. I live it, breathe it, and can never wait to get into the water. One of the ways you can make money through SCUBA is leading tours. Unfortunately, I don't have time to work at a shop full time, but I always try and get involved to earn a few bucks here and there.

Bringing divers out on tours is a great way to earn money and you really don't have to work for a dive shop. All you need is your Divemaster or Instructor certification, experience, and knowledge of the area you and your clients will be diving.

You could make up to $100 per person if you market it correctly and get a good following. Just be sure your clients bring their own gear or that you have a relationship with a shop that can provide you with rental equipment.

Then get out and dive into the underwater world. Just be sure to be safe and follow regulations to the letter.

Motorcycle Lessons

Love to ride? Leather jackets, large handlebars, and long beards are the basis of the motorcycle stigma, but there are lots of other people that ride through the streets.

If you've been riding for a while and can't get enough of the bike then turn your passion into cash and start teaching others how to ride motorcycles. Just get certified and then charge around $400 for a weekend course.

CHAPTER NINE
MAKING MONEY WITH QUIRKY GIGS

Hoop Dance

Sarah Maccarelli Jordan had just left her full-time job as a social worker and felt unfulfilled in her side job as a make-up artist. She wanted to work with kids in some way that positively impact their lives, but how?

One night as luck would have it a hula-hoop fell from the ceiling as she watched her husband's band play a set at a coffee shop. Playing around with the hoop of PVC piping she wondered if there was anything that could be done with such a unique toy.

That is when she discovered hoop dancing. As an old ballet dancer the movement involved came naturally to Sarah and she began to make it into a business.

Creating a Facebook page, instructional Youtube videos, and a website (http://www.hoopingbysarah.com/), she began to perform her art for kids and adults alike. A year later she posted a flyer at a library and that is where the true business began to unfold.

The library asked her to come in and teach classes on hoop dancing to kids and after a successful turn out she was recommended to other libraries. It has now become a way for children to explore movement, get healthy, and have some fun as well as a full on career for Sarah.

Take her story to heart. There's a way to make tons of money doing something that makes you and other's happy. But you have to commit. If starting a business is what you want to do then be my guest and do it, but you have to realize you're in it for the long haul.

Find a PVC pipe, use some rainbow tape, and make yourself a cool hula-hoop and make a child's day.

Mr. Fuzzles the Magic Pet

If you haven't seen this amazing little critter then be wary, when caught it provides endless amounts of laughter and entertainment, the bane of any Scrooge's existence.

At least that's what a young college student named Noah Williams found out when he began to sell Mr. Fuzzles, toy

made out of synthetic string with wire that moves around like a worm in your hands.
(http://www.youtube.com/watch?v=5OJ6iEKtM_Q)

Needing money for extra expenses Noah began to look for something interesting to sell at craft fairs or other such events. Remembering an old magic trick he saw as a kid he looked into the magic worm and found that he could buy a large stock off the internet for about $1.80 a piece.

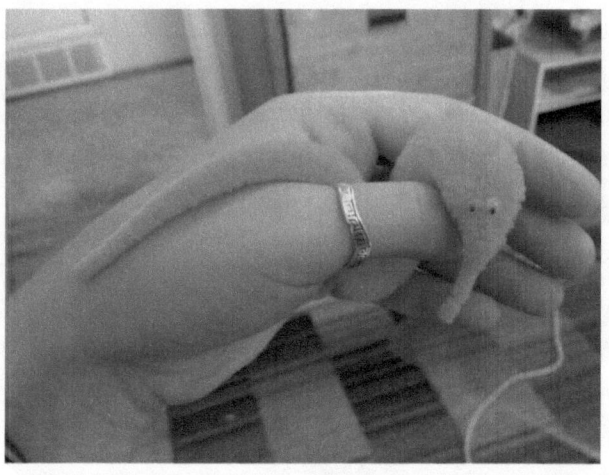

After purchasing a few he began to sell them over the weekends and found that they were immensely popular with young children. On the first go he made over $800 in profit from selling something as simple as a toy.

If you want to make some money as well then find your own Mr. Fuzzles and start selling. All you need to do is be personable and show off how the toy works, a few props are all that's necessary.

Flip for Funds

When people hear the word "flip" they often think of houses. There is great opportunity there, as we have done this a number of times. However, it is also a great opportunity to lose everything, especially all your free time and friendship.

Flipping is simply buying something for one price (hopefully low) and then selling it for another price (hopefully higher.) Many people invest a lot of time, effort and money to find things to flip, but others just develop "a good eye for a bargain."

Using the age old wisdom of "buy low, sell high," you can flip almost anything if you know what you are doing. Often this will give you the seed money to start your own business or provide for a larger income.

If you are going to flip houses with a partner, get everything in writing and make sure that everything is split evenly, including the work hours.

And, You Can Flip Web Domains and Websites.

Andy, a member of our local WordPress meet up, group buys websites that are positioned rightbut need some great SEO and backlinks. In order to monetize them he puts Google adowrds and affiliate links and brings them to a much higher ranking. He then flips them or keeps them as a passive revenue stream.

Another guy in the group watches Google trends and buys up domains before they get popular. He then sells them for a profit, sometimes a big one. If you are good at this, you can triple your money quickly. Or, need I say this, lose your investment.

Police Auctions, Storage Units, Thrift Shop & Yard Sale Treasures

Even if you don't know what you are doing at first, consider it an adventure and set a budget for spending. As you buy wisely you will be able to get "the eye of a treasure hunter." If you blow it and buy junk, you can always donate it and take the donation off your taxes. Or, another friend boxes it up and takes it to the local auction. The auction house takes a cut, but you may come out even.

Buy smart with the goal of immediate re-sell. Do not think it is making you money when it is in a box in the garage. It is costing you seed money that you could be leveraging into a better life for you and your loved ones.

Coin Hunting

Remember our young friend Henry, who cleans carpets and makes money off scrap metal? He also is a coin hunter.

Pre-1982 pennies contain considerable amounts of copper (whearas newer ones are alloyed with zinc to cut costs) and are worth more than a cent apiece. Buy rolls of pennies at the bank, sort them to find older coins, then return the ones you don't want.

Pre-1964 silver half dollars are 90% silver and are worth more than fifty cents apiece. As with pennies, buy rolls of silver dollars at the bank and keep only the most valuable ones.

Tribute Videos for Funerals

Work with funeral directors and church personnel as well as Hospice organizations. Gather photos, memorabilia and testimonials from friends, family and co-workers. Put into a seven minute video that will be played at the funeral and over and over again by the grieving family.

Most families are numb with grief and only knew their loved one in a certain way. It is powerful for them to see how the person impacted the lives of others and will never be forgotten. You can charge from $200-500 for this, simply because of the quick turnaround. You have a limited time to produce a moving tribute to the deceased.

RelayRides: Delivering the Morning Paper

Over the years, the role of the paperboy has changed quite a bit, what started as a neighborhood kid slinging papers from a bike, changed to an adult firing the daily news from a car. Now, with most people getting their news online, even the chance of making a buck putting your car to use has gone the way of the RSS feed.

That said, if you still have a need for some extra cash and have a car, may we suggest that you join RelayRides? You can help make ends meet by renting your car a few times a

month, or make big bucks by renting it more frequently.
And the best part–besides not having to wake up before
dawn to toss newspapers–is that RelayRides protects
owners renting their cars with a $1 million policy.

ReSell Riches

This came in from a friend at http://resalerenegade.com/.

"In reality, I suppose I had always known about reselling.
Ever since I was a child, I was a born entrepreneur. I
remember, as a kid, buying jumbo bags of caramel sour
apple suckers at Costco and selling them off in singles and
doubles for a buck a pop, often times quadrupling my
money or more. It wasn't much, but for a 7th grader, I was
rollin' in the dough! Hustling suckers probably wasn't going
to work in 'real life,' but the principle was the same.

I have a knack for finding value in things that others miss.
That's where the inspiration really came from. That gap is
generally where the fast cash is hiding.

The thing about fast cash, is that you don't generally have
time to plan. If you need cash fast, chances are you need it
now. You have to focus on decisive action. For me, that
meant finding valuable items for free or cheap and turning
them into cold hard cash as soon as possible. I did that a
few ways.

First, I scrapped and recycled. I took to the streets and
found anything metal that I could find on the side of the

road, put it in the back of my truck, and ran it down to the scrap yard. I'm pretty sure I was at the scrap yard every day that week actually. I also asked local businesses if I could recycle their pallets. Often times local businesses will just throw out their pallets because it's too big of a hassle to take them down and get a few bucks for them. For me, though, it was worth it at the time.

At the end of the week I had earned enough money to cover my gas, pay my bills, and give me a little scratch to let my money start earning money for me. It was hard work, though.

My next step was to find imbalances in markets. This meant visiting thrift stores and finding excellent condition items that I could get for pennies, and flipping them on eBay at retail prices.

People seem to have a misconception that they have to find rare or antique items to make great money reselling on eBay. The reality is that there is a monstrous marketplace of shoppers looking for common household goods every day. If you're there to supply those household goods, you get to collect the profit!

The best part is, anyone with a smart phone and the eBay app can find out if there is profit in an item before they even buy it!

CHAPTER TEN
TURNING A GIG INTO A PROFESSION AND A CAREER

Many times what starts out as a fun hobby or special interest rapidly turns into a calling or career. The pleasure that comes from doing something that brings you joy and money is what an optimum life is all about.

A good example is our granddaughter Amanda who has always loved animals. She helped an old man with his cats and in return he volunteered to teach her his business of logging fence posts for the Forest Service.

When she was 14 he started mentoring her about how to cut post and poles and stack the pickup for the maximum capacity. They then sold the load to the local fencing company and made $500 for each delivery.

Seed Money

She took this seed money from working in the woods to buy her first hedgehogs. The first pair was not good breeders and so she kept the female for a pet and bought another female for $250.

They had 4 babies which she raised for 6 weeks and then sold to well-chosen homes for $350 each. Along with a handbook on care and feeding, she is available online and by phone for any questions. Her site is http://www.hedgiesgonecrazy.weebly.com

Creative Types Excel at Entrepreneurship

This comes in from our friends at www.goodbuygirlsnashville.com .

"We met in business school and both had highly successful jobs. The pay and titles were amazing, but we were not allowed to think outside the corporate box. We are both pretty creative but had lots of student loans to pay and needed extra money. People started giving us stuff and we would hit yard sales looking for funky, vintage clothing and stage wear.

"July of 2009 we were making about \$500 a month in our online store. We thought maybe we should find a place to store our stuff. We found a dump but it was only \$350 a month. We took it and moved everything in.

"We used our creative skills to barter websites for construction assistance. At first we were open one day a week, then 3 days a week and then 5 days a week. We still operated the store online and would do all the free advertising we could find. Every single day we would put something on line and share it all over the place.

"We never paid for any advertising, but bartered and traded services and goods with other people who were just getting started in their businesses. Our customers are so great that they tell everyone and got us noticed by some big press.

"Being in Nashville we had made our main focus stage ware, vintage clothing and cowboy boots. We can honestly say that cowboy boots have paid the rent every month.

"GoodBuyGirls has been invited to move into a new concept shopping center and have helped some friends open a men's store similar to ours.

"Our advice is to stay focused on the fun parts and market every day in some way. We are having a great time and the bills get paid by using our creative genius."

Designing Unique Outdoor Gear

Everyone wants something that is unique, awe-inspiring, spectacular, but the only one. Seriously, girls always hate it when that person they hate is wearing a matching shirt to a party, how rude! Well it's the same for outdoor equipment.

Having custom made gear or even little bits and pieces of outdoors paraphernalia are great! Making your own really isn't that hard either and selling it is easier than riding a tricycle. You could paint helmets, sew racing shirts, elaborately decorate bikes, customize water bottles, the ideas are endless. Give someone a series of spectacular adventures with unique products.

TUFA Climbing

Josh Kornish is a young and bright student going to the University of Montana studying Design. The guy now owns a small company he started called TUFA Climbing or Technically Unique Functional Art (https://www.facebook.com/TufaClimbing).

A lover of all things rock climbing Josh started designing chalk bags on his own as a hobby, which has now bloomed into a fully-fledged business.

The story starts out like any dramatic movie. The young climber inherited a hand made chalk bag from a perished older climber, inspiring Josh to create his own unique bag. As he worked on his design he began to make others purchasing different types of materials and machinery.

Soon the business started to branch out due mostly in part to his TUFA Climbing Facebook page that began to gain attention from a number of climbers both near and far.

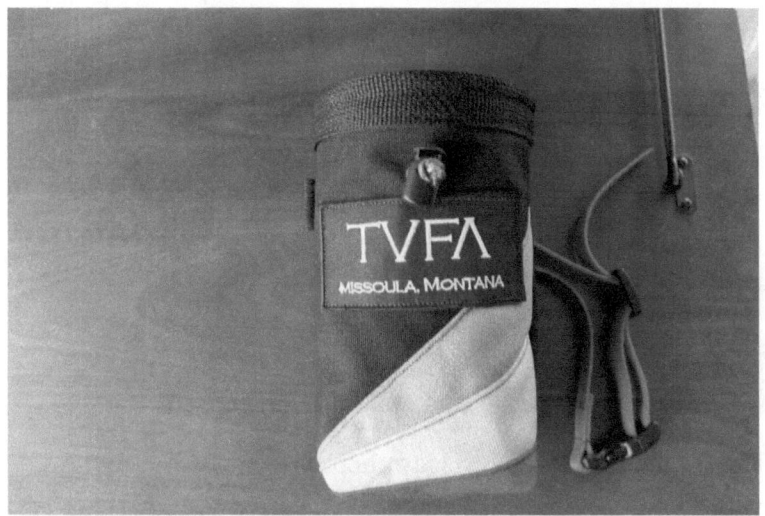

From his experience Josh says that the main obstacle to starting your own business is really yourself. Being able to get over the fear of the unknown world that is before you can be a bit tricky, but taking the leap is the first step to success.

Having help and a passion for the project of course is key too and Josh admits to having a number of friends who give him some great creative advice now and again as well as a passionate drive.

Really the true lesson to learn here is that there is always a way to make some cash and the ones involving passion are usually the most successful.

Sell Your Knowledge

There are many ways to maximize your hard-earned wisdom. Judy teaches writing and Megan teaches scuba diving. Classes are a lot of trouble to organize, market and register on your own. It is easier to go through an adult learning center and let them have a percentage of the fee.

People are willing to pay to learn about many things you know. Just find a niche and become the go-to expert. The greatest attraction to your class is in your title and description, so really spend time developing just the right pitch.

Judy runs Mastermind classes (see http://www.judyhwright.com for more information) and does private coaching in empowerment and personal growth. Life coaching is a thriving business, but you do have to have training and expertise.

Move to Mentor

In one of our successful businesses, "We're Nuts!!!," for cinnamon roasted almonds, our mentor Dick Wood told us to never be discouraged when you go to a show and don't sell too much or the weather is crummy. He said, "If you can't earn, then learn."

Take the time to visit, network, and ask, ask, ask. People love to teach and assist you as you grow your business. Buy them a cup of coffee, help them set up their booth, and then listen to their advice. Be teachable.

CHAPTER ELEVEN
RESOURCES

There are so many government agencies who can help you find work. But you have to be pro-active in finding them and insisting they give you the help and assistance you need in order to be employed. Due to downsizing, many agencies have money to give, but no manpower to advertise or manage it. These services are free. Do not pay to work!

For Veterans

The Department of Labor Veterans Employment and Training Service provides information on job search services available to veterans.

The Veterans Job Bank connects unemployed veterans to job openings with companies that want to hire them. The Obama Administration partnered with leading job search companies to create a new, easy to use online service that enables employers to "tag" job postings for veterans.

It launched with more than 500,000 job listings, a number that will continue growing as more companies tag the job postings on their own websites and add them to the Veterans Job Bank.

Veterans Recruiting Services connects employers and veterans through virtual career fairs. VRS offers services to assist veterans and their spouses as they transition to the civilian workforce, and helps employers find the right highly qualified, educated and well-trained veterans for their businesses.

My Next Move for Veterans is an easy-to-use online tool created by the Department of Labor that allows veterans to enter information about their experience and skills in the field, and match it with civilian careers that put that experience to use. The site also includes information about salaries, apprenticeships, and other related education and training programs.

The Veteran Gold Card provides post-9/11 veterans with extra support as they transition out of the military. Once a veteran has downloaded the Veteran Gold Card, he or she can access six months of personalized case management, assessments and counseling at the roughly 3,000 One-Stop Career Centers located across the country.

Hero 2 Hired (H2H) is a comprehensive employment program provided by the Department of Defense that offers everything a Reserve Component job seeker needs to find their next opportunity, including job listings, career exploration tools, education and training resources, virtual career fairs, a mobile app for IOS, Android and Windows Phones, an innovative Facebook application and a variety of networking opportunities.

H2H also provides vast recruiting opportunities for military-friendly employers, including unlimited free postings; ability to send digital invitations to gauge the interest of potential veteran candidates; automatic notifications for applications; H2H messages and connect requests; and search capabilities on H2H's database to match the qualifications required for positions. h2h.jobs/

The U.S. Chamber of Commerce is committed to Hiring Our Heroes, and are sponsoring 100 hiring fairs for veterans and military spouses in local communities across the country between March 2011-March 2012.

They have also created strategic partnerships to deal with specific populations of veterans and their unique challenges in three other areas to include: a Wounded Warrior Transition Assistance Program, a Post 9-11 Student Veteran Internship and Employment Program, and a Women Veterans and Military Spouses Employment Program.

The Military Spouse Employment Partnership
http://www.msepjobs.com/ (MSEP) is a comprehensive web-enabled recruitment and career partnership solution connecting military spouses to employers seeking a 21st century workforce with the skills and attributes possessed by military spouses.

MSEP provides a digital recruiting platform for vetted FORTUNE 500 PLUS employers who have committed to identifying and promoting career employment opportunities for military spouses, posting job openings on the MSEP web portal, and to offering transferrable, portable careers to relocating military spouse employees.

VetSuccess.gov provides comprehensive transition and employment resources for veterans, service members, and their families. VetSuccess.gov serves as a virtual employment resource center where veterans can browse job listings, post resumes and apply for positions online. VetSuccess.gov also provides links to over 8 million jobs on the VetCentral site.

Services for Job Seekers

The ETA provides services designed to help workers in any phase of their job search.

- **Career Information** - America's Career InfoNet provides information on different careers, employment trends, growing industries and more

- **Youth** - ETA's Youth Programs provide resources for getting young people engaged in training and involved in the workforce

- **Adults** - ETA's Adult Programs provide links to a range of programs providing job search services for Adults

- **Indians and Native Americans** - The Indians and Native American Programs provide information on employment and training opportunities to Native Americans

- **TANF** - The Office of Family Assistance in the Department of Health and Human Services provides information on Temporary Aid for Needy Families

- **Seniors** - The Senior Community Service Employment Program provides part-time employment opportunities for low-income persons aged 55 and older

- **Disabilities** - ETA's disAbility Online Web site provides information on grants and contracts and resources for individuals with disabilities

- **Farm Workers** - The National Farm Worker Jobs Program provides information on employment and training opportunities for migrant and seasonal farm workers

ABOUT THE AUTHORS

Why We Wrote This Book

Judy Helm Wright

Our family has owned and operated many businesses. It is always surprising when young people apply for a position and yet tell me they have never worked before. The ones who have had to create entrepreneurial methods of earning their spending money stand head and shoulders above other candidates.

That was the reason behind my first book *Kids, Chores & More- Teaching Your Kids To Help At Home* (available at http://www.ArtichokePress.com). We could spot the potential employees who had done chores, worked part-time and knew had to problem solve. They got hired. And promoted.

When downsized or underemployed friends complain that
"there are no jobs" I tell them to create one. It is not
societies place to make life easy for you. It is your
responsibility to search out new solutions and to provide
for yourself and loved ones.

If you find yourself with more month than money perhaps
some of ideas will resonate and some will not. Choose one
or two and make a decision to control your own future.
The more you learn, the more you can earn. So, pull up
your bootstraps and start creating your own income.

Judy Helm Wright aka "Auntie Artichoke" a wise woman
with a global message of respect, responsibility and
resilience. To hire Judy as a speaker for your association or
conference please go to http://www.judyhwright.com

Megan Herring

Currently I am an incoming sophomore at the University of Southern California in LA studying Creative Writing and Biology with a little Cinematography on the side. Of course, like every college student in the nation I'm always begging for money. Extra cash translates into concerts, travel, food, and even a ride on the metro.

Parents always complain that they paid their way through college by getting a job flipping burgers or delivering pizza, but it's not that simple anymore. To pay for college on minimum wage you would have to work 11 hour shifts 7 days a week for all four years of school, leaving no time to actually attend classes. So how are we supposed to make it?

That's where this book comes in handy. Sure it may have simple methods that only net a few hundred or so, but fast ways to earn a buck is what college students like me need. Even if it's just to pay for a few good meals or that Muse show at the Staples Center, money is key.

Even writing this book I've found so many ways of getting off of my lazy butt and making some money. I always hear students complaining down the hall of the dorm that they don't have enough saved up for that lab coat or those fancy sneakers.

So college students take this book to heart and instead of reading about Benjamin Franklin, go find his portrait on a crisp bill.

Have you found a great way to earn some extra cash? Then share it with us at info@welcomeabundance.com and be included in the next series of books. You can also find them on the website http://www.ArtichokePress.com.

MOTIVATIONAL QUOTES ABOUT WORK AND ENTREPENEURSHIP

"We all have tremendous potential, and we all are blessed with gifts. Yet, the one thing that holds all of us back is some degree of self-doubt. It is not so much the lack of technical information that holds us back, but more the lack of self confidence."
Robert T Kiyosaki, *Rich Dad Poor Dad*

"The five essential entrepreneurial skills for success are concentration, discrimination, organization, innovation, and communication."
Michael Faraday

"We are shifting from a managerial society to an entrepreneurial society."
John Naisbett

"Jeremy Stoppelman starts Yelp. Max Levchin started Slide. I start Linkedin. It was a mininova explosion of folks jumping out to doing other entrepreneurial activities."
Reid Hoffman

"Create your job! It might sound far-fetched for some of you (while others have already done it) but it's very possible. Not easy, mind you: it takes hard work and smarts and passion and a crap-ton of learning and a willingness to take risks and make mistakes. If that sounds like you, read on. If not, stop reading."
Zen Mind

"Just don't give up trying to do what you really want to do. Where there's love and inspiration, I don't think you can go wrong."
Ella Jane Fitzgerald

"A business absolutely devoted to service will have only one worry about profits. They will be embarrassingly large."
Henry Ford

"Your beliefs become your thoughts, Your thoughts become your words, Your words become your actions, Your actions become your habits, Your habits become your values, Your values become your destiny."
Mahatma Gandhi

"It's not hard to make decisions when you know what your values are."
Roy Disney

"Experience is a hard teacher because she gives the test
first, the lesson afterwards."
Vernon Sanders Law

"You are never given a wish without also being given the
power to make it come true. You may have to work for it,
however."
Richard David Bach

"Genius is 1% inspiration and 99% perspiration.
Accordingly a genius is often merely a talented person who
has done all of his or her homework."
Thomas Edison

"If it wasn't hard, everyone would do it. It's the hard that
makes it great."
Tom Hanks in A League of Their Own

"As surely as the acorn becomes the oak tree, the images in
your mind become your reality."
Unknown

"Start by doing what's necessary, then what's possible; and
suddenly you are doing the impossible."
Saint Francis of Assisi

"Confidence is the result of hours and days and weeks and years of constant work and dedication."
Roger Staubach

"The greatest weariness comes from work not done."
Eric Hoffer

"Hard work is painful when life is devoid of purpose. But when you live for something greater than yourself and the gratification of your own ego, then hard work becomes a labor of love."
Steve Pavlina

"An ant on the move does more than a dozing ox. "
Lao Tzu

"Opportunity is missed by most people because it is
dressed in overalls and looks like work."
Thomas Edison

"We forget that every good that is worth possessing must
be paid for in strokes of daily effort. We postpone and
postpone, until those smiling possibilities are dead."
William James

"Far and away the best prize that life offers is the chance to
work hard at work worth doing."
Thomas Jefferson

"It seems the harder I work, the more luck I have."
Thomas Jefferson

"The healthiest competition occurs when average people
win by putting above average effort."
Colin Powell

"I know you've heard it a thousand times before. But it's
true - hard work pays off. If you want to be good, you have
to practice, practice, and practice. If you don't love
something, then don't do it."
Ray Bradbury

"Hard work spotlights the character of people: some turn up their sleeves, some turn up their noses, and some don't turn up at all. "
Sam Ewing

"If a man is called to be a street sweeper, he should sweep streets even as Michelangelo painted, or Beethoven played music, or Shakespeare wrote poetry. He should sweep streets so well that all the hosts of heaven and earth will pause to say, here lived a great street sweeper who did his job well."
Martin Luther King, Jr.

"I don't wait for moods. You accomplish nothing if you do that. Your mind must know it has got to get down to work."
Pearl S. Buck

"If you can't excel with talent, triumph with effort."
Stephen G. Weinbaum

"Never work just for money or for power. They won't save
your soul or help you sleep at night."
Marian Wright Edelman

"Careers, like rockets, don't always take off on schedule.
The key is to keep working the engines."
Gary Sinise

"Success is peace of mind which is a direct result of self-
satisfaction in knowing you did your best to become the
best you are capable of becoming."
John R. Wooden

"He that would have the fruit must climb the tree."
Dr. Thomas Fuller

"Nobody's a natural. You work hard to get good and then work to get better. It's hard to stay on top."
Paul Coffey

"The only place success comes before work is in the dictionary."
Vincent "Vince" Lombardi

"The heights by great men reached and kept were not attained by sudden flight, but they while their companions slept, were toiling upward in the night."
Henry Wadsworth Longfellow

"All growth depends upon activity. There is no development physically or intellectually without effort, and effort means work."

Calvin Coolidge

"Hard work doesn't guarantee success, but improves its chances."

B. J. Gupta

"Success is dependent on effort."

Sophocles

"If people knew how hard I worked to achieve my mastery, it wouldn't seem so wonderful after all."

Michelangelo

"I know in each moment I am free to decide.
Wayne W. Dyer"

"What would you attempt to do if you knew you could not
fail?"
Dr. Robert Schuller

"I've always felt that if you're not on your side why should
anyone else be. So I always encourage people to be
confident, and sometimes even a little falsely so, just so
you can give yourself an opportunity."
Robert Downey, Jr.

"Lack of Money is the root of all evil."
George Bernard Shaw

"The Wright brothers flew right through the smokescreen
of impossibility."
Charles F. Kettering

"Don't be afraid to take a big step if one is indicated. You
can't cross a chasm in two small jumps."
David Lloyd George

"The only difference between *fear* and *excitement* is what
we label it. The two are pretty much the same
physiological/emotional reaction. With fear, we put a
negative spin on it: "Oh, no!" With excitement, we give it
some positive English: "Oh, boy!"
John-Roger in Life 101

HOW TO MAKE FAST CASH
FUN AND LEGAL WAYS TO EARN MORE MONEY IN A WEEKEND